IMAGES
of America

KINGSTON

IMAGES
of America

KINGSTON

Kingston Historical Society

ARCADIA
PUBLISHING

Published by Arcadia Publishing
Charleston, South Carolina

Printed in the United States of America

Library of Congress Control Number: 2019936586

For all general information, please contact Arcadia Publishing:
Telephone 843-853-2070
Fax 843-853-0044
E-mail sales@arcadiapublishing.com
For customer service and orders:
Toll-Free 1-888-313-2665

Visit us on the Internet at www.arcadiapublishing.com

The Kingston Historical Society dedicates this work to past president Harriet Muhrlein, with our thanks for her many contributions and for zealously safeguarding the town's historical records.

CONTENTS

ACKNOWLEDGMENTS

The Kingston Historical Society (KHS) is grateful to society members and to the many Kingston residents, former residents, visitors, businesses, and organizations that shared their photographs with us and allowed us to reproduce them here. These images and accompanying stories added greatly to our knowledge of Kingston history. We are delighted to have the opportunity to include them in this volume.

The society's publication committee members Kathleen Sole, Deborah L.J. MacKinnon, Michelle Will, Edward Goodwin, Terryl M. Asla, and Suzanne Jenny shared responsibility for researching, scanning images, developing captions, and drafting and editing. The committee wishes to give special thanks to Deborah L.J. MacKinnon for her tireless work compiling the volume and organizing it for publication. Without her dedication and skills, this book would not have been possible. We also wish to thank Arcadia Publishing editors Erin Vosgien and Stacia Bannerman for their support and assistance with this project.

Historical documents use the terms Apple Tree Cove, Appletree Cove, and Apple Cove to describe the Puget Sound inlet at Kingston. For consistency, the term Apple Tree Cove is used throughout this book.

Images credited to KHS are courtesy of the Kingston Historical Society; NKF&R, North Kitsap Fire & Rescue; and VGCC, Village Green Community Center.

INTRODUCTION

Kingston is a small, unincorporated community in Kitsap County on the northern Kitsap Peninsula in western Washington state. Across Puget Sound from Seattle, it lies west of the urban mainland nestled between the Olympic and Cascade Mountain ranges. Kingston is primarily known as the western hub of the Washington State Ferries most direct route to recreation areas in the Olympic National Forest. To access this scenic wilderness of lush rainforests, quiet lakes, towering mountains, and wild ocean beaches, approximately four million people travel through Kingston annually. With its beautiful open harbor extending inland for almost a mile, Kingston provides a calm, safe anchorage for boaters. It also allows a direct water route to the San Juan Islands and Canadian waters—prized tourist destinations for world-class whale watching and sea kayaking.

Over the centuries, Kingston developed a rich history and a unique culture. The town has reinvented itself continually in response to ever-changing circumstances and needs. Tribes canoed in the area before it was discovered by European explorers. With its heavily forested land that descends gently down to the waters of Puget Sound, Kingston later became an ideal site to harvest timber.

On April 24, 1890, two developers, C.C. Calkins of Seattle and Samuel B. Brierly, president of the Kingston Land & Improvement Company, platted the Kingston townsite. They envisioned the town becoming a popular summer resort area, complete with a major hotel and recreation opportunities to rival Monterey Bay, California. The timing was not quite right to attract buyers, however, and Kingston developed more slowly than anticipated. The community entered the 20th century dotted with cabins and homes, where city dwellers enjoyed summer getaways, and small farms and ranches, where a variety of edible crops and beautiful flowers flourished.

Following the Mosquito Fleet era, community residents voted in 1919 to create a port district to improve their dock facilities. As cars became more common on the Kitsap Peninsula, demand increased for car ferries. The Kingston-Edmonds ferry route began in 1923, and a year later, a Kingston-Ballard route was added. The state took over the privately run ferries in 1951; they are administered now as part of the Washington State Department of Transportation.

During Prohibition, rumrunners used Kingston's forested shores to hide illicit Canadian whiskey. In World War II, a US Navy degaussing station was established on the shores of Puget Sound, with cables spanning the water to demagnetize US ships leaving Bremerton and prevent their detection by enemy submarines. Near the end of the war, Kingston was hit with a Japanese balloon bomb intended to start fires in the heavily forested Pacific Northwest. During the Cold War, Kingston housed a military missile defense site to protect Seattle from potential enemy attacks.

The town grew slowly from the late 20th century to the present day. Distinct downtown, midtown, and uptown commercial areas took shape, and residences began to appear along the shore and on the forested hills above town. At the same time, Kingston residents were committed to retaining the natural beauty of the area, with its many trees, trails, streams, creeks, and estuaries. Kingston's public port developed covered and uncovered moorage, guest and fuel docks, two delightful public parks, and a pavilion for local concerts.

While some of these changes altered the look and size of the town, Kingston neighbors today still generally know one another, and shop owners are on a first-name basis with many of their customers. A brief stop at a local store often takes longer than expected because one usually encounters a friend or acquaintance. Over time, the community also seems to retain some key characteristics—chronicled in the chapter titles of this book—that make it unique.

Kingston residents are independent and resilient. As an unincorporated portion of the county, the town does not have a local infrastructure to support its efforts. But residents have made remarkable accomplishments by simply rolling up their sleeves and getting things done. Volunteerism is the hallmark of Kingston, and numerous projects such as the historic two-story Kola Kole schoolhouse and ball field; the Boy Scout cabin; and the Village Green park, picnic pavilion, and children's playground were built with volunteer labor and local monetary contributions.

Additionally, light posts in town are maintained and decorated with hanging flower baskets and holiday decorations each year, supported by contributions from residents and the labor of volunteers. The Fourth of July parade (one of the longest-running parades west of the Mississippi River), Tiny Town children's events, and evening fireworks display always draw huge crowds and are also funded and staffed locally. Numerous events such as food drives, Pie in the Park, Festival of Trees, and others benefit local nonprofit organizations and service clubs, and businesses can be counted on to support or sponsor many community projects.

Remarkably, in 2016, the community completed a 15-year project to raise funds to build and operate the Village Green Community Center. This beautiful 23,000-square-foot building was constructed at a cost of more than $9.1 million. The center houses the Kingston Branch of Kitsap Regional Library, a senior center that is home to numerous activities and programs, the Boys and Girls Club, and three meeting rooms that can be combined to create a banquet hall to seat 200 people. The facility also includes a commercial teaching kitchen, technology lab, and sports court.

Kingston residents have a fun and whimsical spirit. The early town's bathtub and slug races are evidence of their enthusiasm. Today, many events such as the public market and annual Kites Over Kingston, Almost Summer, and Fourth of July celebrations are cherished by locals as well as visitors.

In 2018, a new chapter in the community's history began with the advent of a passenger-only ferry to speed people from the Port of Kingston to downtown Seattle in less than an hour. While the town will surely grow, residents are confident that this change, like many others before it, will not cause Kingston to lose its small-town charm.

The year 2019 seemed a most appropriate time to release this book, as it marks three milestones for Kingston: the Port of Kingston celebrates its centennial, the Kingston Cove Yacht Club observes its 50th anniversary, and the Kingston Public Market opens for its 30th year. Through the photographs and stories in these pages, we hope we have captured some of the flavors of this special place we call home.

One

GATEWAY TOWN

Kingston is in the ancestral territory of the Suquamish People. Apple Cove Point in the Suquamish language is known as *səsxq*, meaning "a whisper" and is where the tribe camped while fishing. The Kingston area is known as *q'ʷəqo'lob*. A third campsite near Carpenter Creek estuary is *q̓aqaxʷac*, meaning "many crabapple trees." The Port Gamble S'Klallam Tribe frequented the area during harvest seasons and canoe travels. In their language, Kingston is *qʷəyəqʷúliʔ*. (Courtesy of Joseph Price.)

To learn more about the Suquamish Tribe, go to suquamish.nsn.us or visit their museum at 6861 NE South Street in Suquamish, Washington. To learn more about the Port Gamble S'Klallam Tribe, please reference *The Strong People: a history of the Port Gamble S'Klallam Tribe* or *Native Peoples of the Olympic Peninsula*. (Postcard image by Ben Benschneider, courtesy of the Suquamish Museum.)

In 1989, Washington celebrated 100 years of statehood. To ensure the centennial represented the First Peoples of Washington, Emmett Oliver, Quinault, founded the Paddle to Seattle. Both S'Klallam and Suquamish members participated in this event and subsequent canoe journeys, including one in 2014 to Bella Bella, British Columbia—a journey of over 500 miles, with 57 participating canoes. (Courtesy of Joseph Price.)

On May 9, 1841, Lt. Charles Wilkes, commander of the first US Exploring Expedition, described the area, later named Kingston, in his log: "This was named Apple Tree Cove, from the number of that tree which were in blossom." At the expedition's end, a military court convicted Wilkes of illegally punishing his men. Some speculate Melville modeled *Moby Dick's* Captain Ahab after Wilkes. (Courtesy of the New York Public Library.)

Continued encroachment of non-Indian settlers led to increased hostility between the tribes and the newcomers. The federal government perceived the need to extinguish Indian title to the land in order to keep peace. In 1855, the tribes and federal government entered into treaties. By 1860, all but 12 Kitsap residents worked for mills. This photograph shows oxen dragging logs down Moe Brothers Skid Road, northwest of Kingston. (Courtesy of KHS.)

In Spring 1853, J.J. Felt built a sawmill at Apple Tree Cove. Finding the cove an undesirable size and depth, Felt moved the mill to Port Madison on Bainbridge Island after the first winter. G.A. Meigs, seen at left, later bought and improved the Port Madison Mill, pictured below in 1890. (Both, courtesy of Bainbridge Island Historical Society.)

On July 11, 1878, W.S. and Caroline Ladd sold their homestead to logger Michael King for $387.50. He threw together a bunk and cookhouse. Some unmarried logging crew likely built a row of shanties. By 1881 or 1882, King had packed up and left, leaving the abandoned buildings to be occupied by out-of-work loggers, squatters, and drifters. The area earned the nickname "King's Town," probably as a joke. Later, it officially became known as Kingston. This picture shows a boom man among logs waiting to be floated to a mill from what is now Arness Park. (Courtesy of Suzanne T. Arness.)

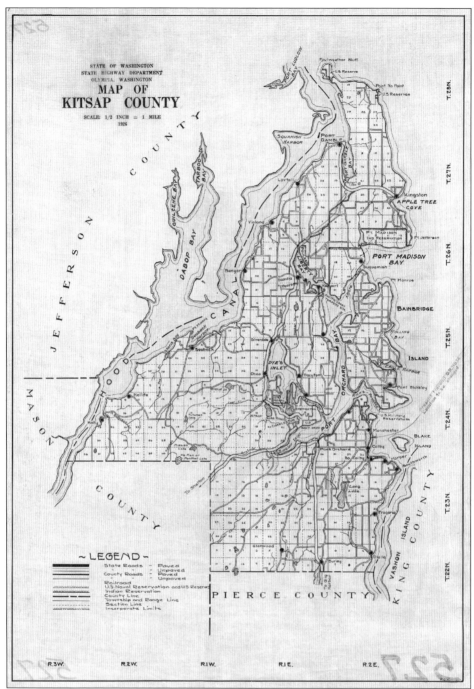

Around 1881, Kitsap County claimed the highest per capita wealth of any county in the country. Five of the world's largest lumber mills shipped their product from its shore. Once the standing timber moved further inland, the expense increased, forcing many shoreline mills to close. Only the Puget Mill of Pope and Talbot in nearby Port Gamble survived. This map shows mostly unpaved roads in Kitsap County in 1926, which were used by diesel trucks to transport logs. (Courtesy of Washington State Archives.)

Barber Cutoff Road began as a railroad right-of-way. Locomotives delivered logs to a large staging area along the waterfront at Apple Tree Cove. A jill poke pushed the logs off the railroad cars one at a time into the bay to be rafted to Ballard. One Kingston man, Robert J. Barry, was killed in an accident involving his "locy." (Photograph from Pope and Talbot Inc., courtesy of KHS.)

Early Kingston Historical Society members recall the old log staging area as the largest cleared area in town. Woods covered everything else. The school used the staging area for picnics. Even a circus, like the Douglas Shows caravan shown here in 1936, used the area to entertain the community. (Courtesy of KHS.)

Seattle developer C.C. Calkins dreamed of Kingston as a resort hideaway for Seattle folk. Along with Samuel B. Brierly, Calkins platted the Kingston townsite in April 1890. (Courtesy of KHS.)

Samuel B. Brierly served as president of the Kingston Land & Improvement Company. This image, taken from a larger photograph seen on page 77, is believed to be of Brierly and is the only known photograph of him. (Courtesy of KHS.)

As early as April 24, 1890, developers dubbed Kingston the "Jewel City of Puget Sound" and the "Monterey of Washington." Advertisements, like this one circulated in Seattle, claimed that Kingston had "one of the finest views . . . found in the entire state of Washington." Developers touted the new town an ideal spot for a getaway from the cares of the world. (Courtesy of Washington State History Museum.)

The Puget Mill Company owned much of the land surrounding Kingston's Apple Tree Cove, which held back the development of the community to some extent. The above photograph shows downtown Kingston around 1890. Eventually, Kingston lots were put on the market. Below, Central Avenue can be seen in 1918, just prior to the establishment of the port district in 1919. The pier where Mosquito Fleet steamers docked can be seen. On the left is Breakey's store with a wagon filled with supplies parked out front. (Both, courtesy of KHS.)

By late 1887, Ole Hauan bought 35 acres at Apple Tree Point from Charles I. Richards for $200. Later, Hauan supplied the Outing Club, a camp organized by University of Washington professors in 1906, with supplies. Hauan rowed out regularly to transport goods and people from boats that could not come ashore. He sold his property to Von V. Tarbill for $3,000 in 1925. (Painting by Rick Eveleth.)

During Prohibition, rumrunners used Kingston as one of their drop-off spots. Ole Hauan estimated he had rescued about 35 rumrunners from the water. Only one person, a Japanese sailor who purposely jumped overboard, ever expressed gratitude. Longtime Kingston resident Jim Thompson identified Bud Clark (pictured here) and Pop Fuller as local bootleggers. Residents referred to a local creek as "Pop Fuller Creek" at one time. (Courtesy of Tim Burns.)

At right, Dr. Vernon L. Parrington and his wife, Julia, wade in the waters of Apple Tree Cove. Dr. Parrington, a distinguished professor at the University of Washington (UW), won a Pulitzer Prize in 1928. The couple participated in the Outing Club, a popular summer camp for professors and their families from 1906 to 1931. It occupied 31 acres on Apple Tree Point. Below, children of the Outing Club sit in a boat in the early 1920s. From left to right are Louise Parrington, Marian Lucas, Eunice Padelford, and Annabell Hall. (Both, courtesy of Sarah Parrington.)

Donald P. Thomas made the drawing of the Padelford cabin seen above. His father taught architecture at the University of Washington and would have participated in the Outing Club. Both Dr. Parrington and Dr. Padelford have buildings named in their honor on the UW campus in Seattle. The photograph below features Dick O'Dell and his three sons (from left to right), Rick, Mike, and Steve, in 1965 enjoying a day at the beach off President Point. The cabins in the background were likely used by summer residents in the 1930s. (Above, drawing by Donald P. Thomas, courtesy of Sarah Parrington; below, courtesy of Shelley Worrall.)

Apple Tree Point offered rental cabins built by Von V. Tarbill. The obelisk-like structure to the right in the picture above is a lighthouse. It consisted of pilings pushed together with a light at the top. Not a standard lighthouse, it functioned more like a signal light. The 1930 photograph below provides a different angle, with the navigation light offshore. (Above, courtesy of Sarah Parrington; below, photograph by Betty Tarbill Bosanko, courtesy of KHS.)

In 1900, R.O. Worthington lived in Kentucky with his wife and three children, where he dealt in furniture. Around 1907, he moved his family west and purchased the Kingston Hotel. The 1910 census shows Worthington as a widowed hotel proprietor, living with his daughter and the hotel cook, Cora Carry. In 1913, Worthington and his second wife renovated the 1890 hotel by adding indoor bathrooms and a raised porch, as featured in the 1925 photograph above. Cora Carry, a former slave and Kingston's first black resident, does not appear on the 1920 census. Antoine and Tania Issa bought the hotel in 2016, seen at left in 2018. (Above, courtesy of KHS; left, courtesy of Judith Ryan.)

Two

INDEPENDENT AND
RESILIENT RESIDENTS

Benjamin B. Bannister, originally from England, and Charles I. Richards, his business partner, first settled on Apple Tree Point in 1870. They cleared away the wild crabapple trees, built a cabin, and planted a garden. They lived on the abundance of game and berries. The two men worked in logging in the summer, and during the winter, they produced handmade shingles that they used as legal barter. Known as the "Father of Kingston," Bannister married and raised a family of seven children in Kingston. He counted Jim Sealth, son of Chief Seattle, and Chief Jacobs of the Suquamish Tribe as his personal friends. Bannister Street bears his name. (Photograph from Eleanor Elkins, courtesy of KHS.)

Sam Dawson arrived around 1880 and built his home on the south shore of Apple Tree Cove. He rowed to Port Madison on Bainbridge Island once a week to retrieve mail and to transfer passengers disembarking from Mosquito Fleet boats ashore for 25¢ each. Dawson helped organize the Kingston School District in 1888. He married his wife, Mary (according to census documents), pictured below, in the 1890s. In 1910, Sam drowned, and Mary, who was both deaf and blind, lived with her daughter Annie Seatter. Mary died in 1915. (Both photographs from Tad Parrington, courtesy of KHS.)

Bob Lair, the village "smithy," operated a gas station in the 1920s that Ralph H. Carlaw remodeled in the 1930s. It became Paul Nichol's Farm Store in the 1950s and 1960s and the Holding Lane Tavern in the late 1990s. It is now the Filling Station Bar and Grill. Lair enjoyed renown as a storyteller, blacksmith, and machinist. He supplied Pope and Talbot Mill with the sleds for their donkey engines and built the first logging truck in Kitsap County. Folks claimed whatever Bob built "might not be pretty, but it would last forever." He is pictured to the right with his "motorcycle saw." Below, he stands on the left with his trusted dog Blackie and Cecil VanKeuren. (Right, courtesy of KHS; below, photograph from Jim Harmon and Jan Brill, courtesy of KHS.)

95

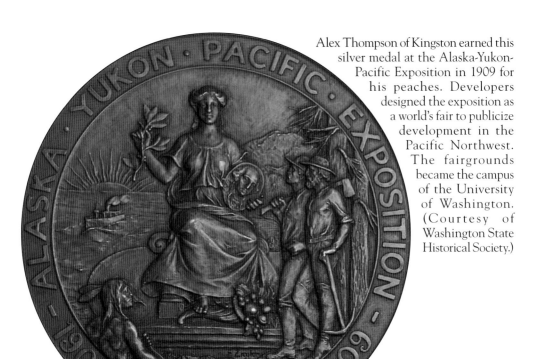

Alex Thompson of Kingston earned this silver medal at the Alaska-Yukon-Pacific Exposition in 1909 for his peaches. Developers designed the exposition as a world's fair to publicize development in the Pacific Northwest. The fairgrounds became the campus of the University of Washington. (Courtesy of Washington State Historical Society.)

Jack Minert, an original Kingston Historical Society member, recalled many family "stump ranches." Farmers left the logged-off stumps in place and worked around them, keeping gardens and raising cows, pigs, and chickens to supplement their work at the mill. (Courtesy of Jo Nelson.)

Originally from Burien, Lynn and Maxine Murray purchased 20 acres in Kingston on top of Shorty Campbell Road for a more rural lifestyle. During the 1960s, they cultivated six acres of dahlias, growing 600 varieties. Visitors came to view the blooms each August, with crowds being especially large during the 1962 Seattle World's Fair. During the wintertime, the Murrays harvested the bulbs and prepared them for mailing in March. Bulbs were sent far and wide. (Courtesy of Jo Nelson.)

A 1962 World's Fair official presents Robert P. Smiley with a plaque honoring Kingston. Smiley, the unofficial mayor of Kingston, is on the left, with his daughter Diane standing behind him. (Courtesy of KHS.)

Jack Minert remembered picking strawberries and cherries as a schoolboy during the summers on local farms. Owens Cherry Orchard, located on property north of what is now Gordon Elementary, would hire seasonal workers from Seattle. Clay Andre's grocery store, pictured above around 1926, sold peaches for $1.35 a crate. From left to right are Clay Andre, Iva Hagerup, and Ernie Stevenson, the clerk. The Kingston Co-op Fruit Growers organized in 1890. Cathy Wartes, Mary McClure, and Marcia Adams started the Kingston Public Market in 1989 at Mike Wallace Marina Park. (Above, photograph from Willa Tate, courtesy of KHS; below, courtesy of KHS.)

This c. 1920 bird's-eye view of Kingston appears to have been taken from Third Street and Iowa Avenue. Though it shows several two-story residences, it also illustrates the degree to which the downtown area was clear cut. (Photograph from Betty HasBrouck, courtesy of KHS.)

In addition to building many of Kingston's original structures, Sam Arness raised chickens for a time. His daughter Helen, the ninth of ten children, collected 30 dozen eggs a day along with completing her homework. Cartons of eggs went out to multiple locations. Helen gladly gave up the task when the chickens stopped laying. (Courtesy of Helen Arness Lawson.)

After the Newell's Kingston Shingle Company closed, the family ran the Newellhurst dairy farm, shown above. Throughout the 1950s, George Newell bred racehorses. A federal investigation into George's partner, Teamster leader Frank Brewster, forced him to sell his beloved horses. The Newellhurst farm fell into disrepair, and the fire department used it for a practice burn sometime in 1965–1966. The Newell family legacy appears on many street signs off Jefferson Point Road. (Above, photograph from June Gasparovich, courtesy of KHS; below, courtesy of NKF&R.)

The Kitsap Bank property on Highway 104 originally housed George's Corner, a store operated by Bennie and Martha George from 1928 to 1941. The couple is pictured here in 1950. Martha loved baseball and served as a faithful scorekeeper. Later in life, she served as Suquamish tribal chairman. Early entrepreneurs, the George family is regarded as a heritage family by Kitsap County. (Courtesy of Ted George.)

After 1941, residents continued to call the intersection of Highway 104 and Miller Bay Road "George's Corner." Today, many also call it "Kingston Crossing." In this photograph, the Kingston Fire Department is conducting a drill at the intersection in 1963. At center, Fire Chief Harold "Teen" Elkins instructs fireman Jerry Cooper, second from left. The others are unidentified. (Courtesy of NKF&R.)

In 1895, the one-room school (right) was built; it remained in operation until 1909. Sam Arness then constructed the two-story building nearby and painted it green and cream. It contained classes until 1951, when it was ceded to Kitsap County. A former Suquamish tribal leader suggested the name Kola Kole, a Salish word meaning "Place of Coming Together." Kingston Cooperative Preschool currently occupies the space. (Courtesy of Suzanne T. Arness.)

Bertha Long prepares to drive kids home from school around 1920. Her preschool-age daughter, Lois, sits second behind her mother in the dark stocking cap. A teenage Sandy Thompson waves them goodbye at right. Bertha's great-granddaughters Cindy Long Larson and Gayle Long drive school buses today. (Photograph from Lois Long Foster, courtesy of KHS.)

In its history, Kingston School District refused admittance to Port Gamble S'Klallam students—except for the children of Bennie and Martha George. Their son Ted George became a national Native American advocate during the Johnson, Nixon, and Ford administrations. He argued for closure of the Indian boarding school system and helped craft a 1987 church apology to Native Americans. Here, Ted stands with classmate Mary Page at a reunion. (Courtesy of Ted George.)

Gordon Elementary bears the name of Richard Gordon, who grew up as a friend of Ted George. Gordon served as an astronaut on Gemini 11 and Apollo 12, as well as an executive for the NFL New Orleans Saints and in the oil and gas industries. Gordon appears second from left, with (from left to right) his brother Norman, his sister Barbara Pethick, and Kingston resident Cheryl Steele. (Courtesy of Cheryl Steele.)

David Henry Wolfle, an immigrant, faced language and educational challenges in addition to a physical deformity caused by a childhood injury. Serving as Kitsap County superintendent from 1928 to 1938, Wolfle established a school at Little Boston on the Port Gamble S'Klallam reservation in 1936. The school survived until 1951, when school buses began bringing children to the first David Wolfle Elementary School. Above, Wolfle is pictured on the left in 1931. June Breiland, as a young girl, stands at center with her father, Nels Virkelyst. Below, the original Wolfle Elementary is pictured in 1986. The current building opened in 1990. (Above, courtesy of Poulsbo Historical Society; below, courtesy of North Kitsap School District.)

Though Kingston is a hub for boats and motor vehicles, it has not been so lucky for aircraft. Sometime between the two world wars, a private plane made an emergency landing in Sam Arness's field on Tulin Road after suffering engine trouble. It appears dangerously close to the family home. Arness stands at far right in his Sunday best; the others are unidentified. (Courtesy of Helen Arness Lawson.)

In 1974, helicopter pilot Dwight Brousseau, 25 years old, crashed upside down in front of an Ohio Avenue home. A courier for American Marine Bank, he took off for Seattle on his daily run but turned back because of fog. Unfortunately, he was killed in the crash. With canceled checks scattered over a half-mile area, the bank stated that the people who turned out to help were wonderful. (Courtesy of NKF&R.)

In 1981, Kingston residents witnessed a small plane crash near Carpenter Lake. At left, the wing of the plane is visible. This was also the year that the 911 system was established in the community. Ten years later, on Feb. 16, 1991, a small plane made an emergency landing using West Kingston Road as a runway (below). The plane had circled George's Corner but could not use Bond Road due to high traffic. The flight, which originated in Alaska, apparently ran out of fuel and had already landed before the FAA notified local authorities. After refueling, the pilot and his two young passengers continued on to SeaTac airport. (Left, courtesy of NKF&R; below, courtesy of Jo Nelson.)

Several local businesses have suffered losses due to fires. In 1978, Drifter's Tavern, seen here, sustained a total loss, along with Frank Johnson Realty next door. Martha "Happy" DeCoteau lamented the loss of Drifter's: "There goes seven years of my life." Known as the "Mother of Kingston" because everyone knew her, DeCoteau then joined the Kingston Inn as a cook, where she worked for over 20 years. (Courtesy of NKF&R.)

On June 29–30, 1990, fire destroyed Kingston's main shopping center, including Olympic Red Apple Market, Apple Tree Pharmacy, Kingston Post Office, the state liquor store, and Kingston Medical Center. Richard Bjarnson, owner of the shopping mall, immediately began rebuilding, while citizens started a relief fund for employees left without work. The new mall houses the Food Market, Kingston Post Office, and Henery's Hardware along with other local businesses. (Courtesy of NKF&R.)

Before it was destroyed in 2005, the Kingston Inn, pictured above, attracted residents as a favorite local gathering place. Lines frequently went out the door, especially on prime rib nights. Below is the Kingston Inn the morning after the September 20, 2005 fire. Two large kitchen vents can be seen in the largest part of the remaining roof. After standing vacant for over a decade, the property was opened as the Port of Kingston Kiwanis Park in 2018. (Both, courtesy of KHS.)

Some of Kingston's early downtown structures have housed multiple tenants. One example is Majestic Coffee Roasters (right). Built in Seattle in 1873, it was brought over by boat to Apple Tree Cove. The building was moved into town in 1906 and functioned as Hyggen's general store. Once a beauty parlor operated by Alfie Williams, Randy and AnneMarie Olson remodeled it and operated the Coffee Exchange from 1993 until it became Majestic Coffee. Father and son Ray and Noah Schloss bought the business in August 2018. Another historic building that now houses Sweet Life Cakery was erected in 1930. The cottage (below) functioned as Vi's Café, an eight-stool café owned by Vi and Charlie Weaver in the 1950s. (Right, courtesy of KHS; below, photograph by Roy Alexander, courtesy of Carrie McLaughlin.)

Robert P. Smiley bought all of the block 94 plat of Kingston. Over his lifetime, he started 13 different businesses in town. Both photographs on this page show his wrecking yard and auto sales business in 1950. The same property today houses Kingston Mini Storage, the Grub Hut, and the Country Pet Shoppe. (Both, courtesy of the Smiley family.)

Three

THRIVING PORT ON
A PROTECTED COVE

Before Kitsap County had good roads and bridges, private transportation companies ran steamers, sternwheelers, sailing ships, and small powerboats to move passengers and freight around Puget Sound. At times, these boats swarmed Puget Sound "as thick as mosquitos" in the eyes of locals, becoming known as the Mosquito Fleet. Pictured here, the steamer *Monticello* exemplified the 20th-century Mosquito Fleet craft. (Photograph from Roland Carey, courtesy of KHS.)

22

Robert Forsyth, one of a family of five unmarried adults, arrived in Kingston from Scotland before 1890. He logged and farmed successfully. Shortly after 1900, he provided the lumber and otherwise financed the first Kingston pier. He lived on the east side of Hansville Road about a mile north of the intersection of State Highway 104 and Miller Bay Road/ Hansville Road. (Photograph from Lucille Weisenberger, courtesy of KHS.)

Also from Scotland, William "Scotty" Seatter arrived in the late 1880s. In addition to managing his South Kingston farm, he served as a watchman on the ships of the Puget Sound Navigation Company, the Black Ball Line. Seatter Road bears his name. (Photograph from George Andresen, courtesy of KHS.)

The *Dode*, seen here, earned a reputation as a workhorse on the Seattle-Kingston-Hood Canal route. The ship's builder named her for his wife, Dora Wells Troutman, who became the first female ship captain on Puget Sound. She eventually served as skipper of the *Dode*. (Photograph from George Andresen, courtesy of KHS.)

Decorated Mosquito Fleet vessels line a busy Kingston dock on July 4, 1910, waiting for visitors to either disembark or load for their return trip. Kingston has always been a premier destination on the Fourth of July. (Photograph from Betty HasBrouck, courtesy of KHS.)

Scene of Kingston, Wash.

At one time, Kingston had three docks: a north dock at Apple Tree Point, a dock at the foot of the town's main street, and a south dock at the foot of what is now Seatter Road. In the early 20th century, the town became a popular stop because it had a sheltered harbor, one of the few between Port Townsend and Seattle. Above, a lone man walks into town on the main dock. At left is the main dock in 1930. At the far end on the left is the car ferry ramp, with newly installed electric overhead lights. The sign on the right reads, "The Little City by the Sea, A Good Place to Buy a Home." (Above, courtesy of KHS; left, courtesy of Sarah Parrington.)

Frank Newell operated the Kingston Shingle Company, Kingston's largest employer from about 1903 to 1915. In 1910, R.M. Newell built the south dock, pictured above in 1922, to bring in passengers and freight for the shingle mill and for homes in the South Kingston area. All that remains of the dock today are the concrete pilings pictured below. (Above, photograph from W.O. Reynolds, courtesy of KHS; below, courtesy of Rick Eveleth.)

The Kingston Port District formed in 1919, creating a public dock at the end of the main street. Car ferry service from Edmonds began in 1923, with the 12-car ferry *City of Edmonds* operated by the Joyce brothers. Commuters paid 25¢ each way as a passenger or $1.50 for a car and driver. The crossing took 45 minutes. Above, cars drive through Kingston after getting off the ferry soon after 1923. By 1925, the Joyces were operating two boats serving the Edmonds route, and Harry Crosby owned and operated a run to Ballard using a smaller boat. The photograph below from 1925 shows cars in two ferry lines; one on the right for those heading to Ballard and another on the left for service to Edmonds. (Above, courtesy of KHS; below photograph from Eleanor Elkins, courtesy of KHS.)

The photograph above from the early 1920s shows a quiet downtown Kingston in between sailings, with no cars lined up. On the left is Kingston Market Meat & Groceries with the slogan "Plenty for All." A child can be seen bicycling across the street. In contrast, the picture below is from 1965, when cars would stretch up Highway 104, nearly blocking it completely. The port added a large holding lot in 1967. The tavern and restaurant below are now a parking lot and Aviators Coffees and Teas. (Both, courtesy of KHS.)

In 1952, Kingston undertook a major engineering project, bringing salt water silt in by dredge pump to fill in some areas around the cove. Manson Construction and Engineering Company had the main contract. Above, Ed Arness is leveling the silt as a sub-contractor. Construction of a new ferry dock was finished in six months. Below is another view of the project. (Above, photograph by C.L. Edwards, courtesy of Suzanne T. Arness; below, courtesy of Juanita Moon Martin.)

This 1963 aerial photograph shows a ferry docked at the Port of Kingston. This view illustrates the shoreline from Apple Tree Cove on the left to Saltair Beach on the right. Shortly after, in 1967, the US Army Corps of Engineers built the breakwater, dredged the harbor, and used the fill to construct what is now the marina, Mike Wallace Marina Park, and the Washington State Department of Transportation ferry terminal and parking lot. (Courtesy of KHS.)

The SS *San Mateo*, the last steamer ferry, finished her 47-year career on Labor Day 1969. Hundreds of passengers rode the Kingston-Edmonds route that day. Built in 1922, she was added to Capt. Alexander Peabody's Black Ball fleet in 1941 for Puget Sound service. Riders adored her unique engine, her quaint whistle, and her stained-glass windows. (Courtesy of the Ralph White Collection, Kitsap Regional Library.)

Car ferry service started on May 17, 1923, with the *City of Edmonds* running from Kingston to Edmonds. It proved so popular that the Joyce brothers, who owned the service, promptly built the *City of Kingston*, seen here, a near replica of the first boat, to begin service in May 1924. (Courtesy of the Ralph White Collection, Kitsap Regional Library.)

The Kingston Cove Yacht Club (KCYC) was founded in 1968–1969. Club member Laura Zetterberg painted the above picture in 1994 in honor of the club's 25th anniversary. Bill Reynolds, former Kingston Historical Society president, made the large KCYC letters adorning the existing clubhouse, constructed in 1995. The letters have since been moved from the roof to the lawn. (Above, painting by Laura Zetterberg, courtesy of KHS; below, courtesy of KHS.)

At 4:40 a.m. on June 9, 1969, Selma Steele reported a fire blazing at the Kingston dock, above. Little did she know that robbers had held her husband, Art, a ferry tollbooth worker, at gunpoint shortly before the fire began. The robbers demanded that Art open the safes. He only opened his, so they set fire in front of the bank of safes, seen below, in the waiting room. Police apprehended the crooks because they ran out of gas in their stolen getaway car. (Above, photograph by Edna Miller; both, courtesy of NKF&R.)

Frank DeBoer, one of the 80 firefighters who responded to the 1969 dock fire, credited the US Coast Guard with getting under the dock to extinguish the blaze, as seen here. Sonny Woodward, who also worked the fire under the dock, explained that the creosote pilings made the fire very difficult to extinguish. (Photograph by Maxine Minert, courtesy of NKF&R.)

Another angle of the fire shows fire trucks spread out across the ferry lanes and the toll booth on the left. In the early years, the dock burned frequently until asphalt replaced the more combustible materials. (Photograph by James F. Perine, courtesy of NKF&R.)

In 1922, the SS *Virginia V*, the last of the authentic Mosquito Fleet steamers, made her maiden voyage. She is now housed at the Museum of History and Industry in Seattle. In 1980, a total of 240 supporters of the Kingston Fireman's Association celebrated aboard the *Virginia V* until the engine quit. Gale force winds tossed the historic steamer around until it could be rescued by the *Walla Walla* ferry. Ironically, North Kitsap Fire & Rescue came to the aid of the *Virginia V* in 2002 when she got hung up in the cove. (Above, courtesy of Virginia V. Foundation; below, courtesy of KHS.)

The Port of Kingston is an anchor for the community, promoting activities and services that bring people to the downtown area, including several parks. Named in 1992, Mike Wallace Park, adjacent to the port offices, stages Concerts in the Park during the summer and other events throughout the year. Cy Wyse, co-founder of Kingston Kiwanis, is pictured at right installing a marker for the park that is now identified as Mike Wallace Marina Park. The picture below shows a concert in the park with a band performing. In 1997, the Port of Kingston purchased the North Beach, also known as Saltair Beach, just north of the ferry terminal and made it accessible for public use. For homecoming, members of Kingston High School parade from the Village Green to Mike Wallace Marina Park. (Right, courtesy of Stephanie Bento; below, courtesy of Kathy Sole.)

Gov. Gary Locke (seated) signs a passenger-only ferry bill in 1998. Kingston residents watch as the governor places his signature on the document. At far right is Billie Johnson, and in front of him is Rosalee Waggoner. Behind Governor Locke in the back row is Sonny Woodward, and also in the back row is Randy Monlux, in glasses. (Courtesy of KHS.)

A fast, passenger-only ferry route to downtown Seattle held much promise, but several early attempts failed due to low ridership. The first efforts, the *Red Head*, the *Aqua Express*, and the *Soundrunner*, could not turn a profit. The Taco Bell seen here in the background is now Cup & Muffin. (Courtesy of KHS.)

Contractor Rick Lanning donated both time and materials to the reinstallation of the old ferry clock. Originally installed in the 1900s, the clock failed to keep accurate time and fell into disuse. George Pease, a master restorer of large clocks, renovated the mostly forgotten clock. He added a final touch, the name "Kingston" in gold letters. The clock is now a signature landmark in the Port of Kingston Kiwanis Park, the port's newest park, dedicated in 2018. (Both, courtesy of the Port of Kingston.)

MV *Finest*, the latest Kingston-Seattle fast ferry, made her first trip to Kingston on November 5, 2018, as captured in the picture below. Gov. Jay Inslee and other dignitaries dedicated the Kitsap Transit vessel on November 19, and her regular schedule began on November 26, 2018. MV *Finest* has the capacity to carry up to 350 passengers on the route to downtown Seattle, which takes 39 minutes. The photograph above shows the *Finest* in her slip, in the fog, before leaving Kingston. (Both, courtesy of the Port of Kingston.)

Four

STRATEGIC MILITARY IMPORTANCE

John Henry Burns Jr. is pictured in his World War I uniform posing with his parents, John Sr. and Lillian. He served in the 1st Infantry Division. While in France, during the battle of St. Mihiel, he endured exposure to mustard gas but suffered no major problems. The military reassigned him to the 28th Infantry Division in Eschelbach, Germany. He returned home in 1919. Local lore claims the community honored World War I vets by planting trees in front of Kola Kole when it was the grade school. (Courtesy of Tim Burns.)

For the United States, World War II started with the bombing of Pearl Harbor on December 7, 1941. Kingston suffered its first loss that day when a bomb took the life of Donald J. Mathison, nicknamed "Chewy," aboard the USS *West Virginia*, shown here. David Berg received a Distinguished Flying Cross citation for his participation in dive-bombing attacks during the Battle of Midway in 1942. The military declared him dead in June 1943. Walt Parcells survived being shot down over Italy twice. (Courtesy of the Library of Congress.)

UNITED STATES OF AMERICA
OFFICE OF PRICE ADMINISTRATION

434642 EM

O.P.A.
VALID
U.S.A.

WAR RATION BOOK No. 3

Void if altered

NOT VALID WITHOUT STAMP

Identification of person to whom issued: PRINT IN FULL

Robert P. Smiley

(First name)   (Middle name)   (Last name)

Street number or rural route *Star Route*

City or post office *Suquamish*   State *Wash.*

AGE	SEX	WEIGHT	HEIGHT	OCCUPATION
28	*male*	130 Lbs.	5 Ft. 4¼	*and*

SIGNATURE *Robert P Smiley*

(Person to whom book is issued. If such person is unable to sign because of age or incapacity, another may sign in his behalf.)

WARNING

This book is the property of the United States Government. It is unlawful to sell it to any other person, or to use it or permit anyone else to use it, except to obtain rationed goods in accordance with regulations of the Office of Price Administration. Any person who finds a lost War Ration Book must return it to the War Price and Rationing Board which issued it. Persons who violate rationing regulations are subject to $10,000 fine or imprisonment, or both.

OPA Form No. R-130

LOCAL BOARD ACTION

Issued by _____

(Local board number)   (Date)

Street address _____

City _____   State _____

(Signature of issuing officer)

Robert P. Smiley grew up in Texas and served eight years in the US Navy, stationed in the South Pacific. Six weeks before the attack on Pearl Harbor, he moved his family to Washington. While he worked on torpedoes at Naval Torpedo Station Keyport, the family managed—as families did—using war ration books. His ration book is pictured here. His address appears as Suquamish though he lived north of the current Wolfle Elementary School. (Courtesy of the Smiley family.)

79

Yoko and Toshisaburo Fukuzawa (pictured in 1959) came to Kingston in the 1920s, farming strawberries with great success. In 1942, the government interned them at Tule Lake Relocation Center, along with seven other Japanese families from Kingston. They remained there until the end of the war, returning to Kingston with only one other Japanese household. (Photograph from Alfie Williams and Yukie Fukuzawa Yamibe, courtesy of KHS.)

The Parcells sisters are, from left to right, Marion, Lois, Ethyl, Ruth, and Ruby. Ruth and Ruby enlisted in the US Cadet Nurse Corps in 1944. The US Public Health Services trained the cadets, 17- to 35-year-old women who came from all backgrounds. They received a subsidy in exchange for a pledge to serve for the duration of the war, guaranteeing the country had enough nurses at home and abroad. Ruby could not serve due to a heart murmur. Ruth, however, trained in hospitals in Tacoma and Seattle before nursing in Bremerton. (Courtesy of Marrion Dennis.)

The school bus would not drive on unnamed roads, so the young Parcells sisters had to walk two miles to the bus stop. When their father officially named it Parcells Road, the bus came right into their yard to pick them up. This 1962 photograph shows Kingston Farm Road, which branched off Parcells Road, likely named for a large farm at the end of the road. (Courtesy of Sarah Parrington.)

Von V. Tarbill bought 23 acres on Apple Tree Point in 1925 while an economics professor at the University of Washington. He died in 1937, leaving his wife, Margaret, to care for the family farm. In March 1945, Margaret and her youngest daughter, Katie, received a call in Seattle that their Kingston property was on fire. When they arrived at the farm, FBI agents explained the fire was caused by a Japanese firebomb and required that no one speak of it. The government did not want the Japanese to know their bombs had succeeded. Von and Margaret Tarbill are pictured here in 1916. (Courtesy of Katie Tarbill Fortune.)

When 11-year-old Katie Tarbill, seen here, arrived with her mother to witness the Japanese firebomb's damage to their property, she found a dozen neighbors fighting the blaze with a bucket brigade. Eventually, they had to use shovelfuls of sand to put it out. Sand made up most of Apple Tree Point. (Courtesy of Katie [Tarbill] Fortune.)

Katie (Tarbill) Fortune displays her 1957 painting of the family's property. Today, million-dollar homes have replaced the small cottages, and wetlands exist where the firebomb landed. (Courtesy of Suzanne Jenny.)

During World War II, a degaussing station was on President Point Road. It monitored equipment placed in Puget Sound to neutralize magnetic fields in military ships and to reduce their vulnerability to enemy attack. It later became a private residence, and in the 1980s, sheltered an exotic bird farm. (Courtesy of KHS.)

Lynn Hammond, a salon owner and longtime resident, remembers her son running into their house in 1988, excitedly declaring, "Mom, I've just seen the biggest duck in the whole world!" In fact, a swan had gotten loose from the exotic bird farm and leisurely floated the waters of the cove. It may have been looking for a mate. (Painting by Rick Eveleth.)

The land known as Quiet Place Park, west of Ohio Avenue and above Fourth Street, originally belonged to Col. Richard Elvins and his wife, Naomi. In 1946, the US Army purchased an easement so it could cut trees and brush for sight clearance in conjunction with Seattle Defense Area Battery S-92-C. This may have been to protect microwave communications with the battery control site at Fort Lawton. (Courtesy of Mark E. Libby.)

Between 1954 and 1974, the Cold War brought missiles to Kingston. The Army strategically located these ground-to-air missiles to protect against attacks by enemy bombers. The current high school complex on Siyaya Avenue, running north of West Kingston Road, occupies the old missile launch site. In June 1958, the Kingston Nike Ajax battery was replaced with Nike Hercules missiles. In this image, young residents look at a Nike Hercules missile with awe as it makes its way through town. On the far right is a young Bob Smiley. All others are unidentified. (Courtesy of KHS.)

The former Nike control headquarters on Ohio Avenue are now occupied by the Northwest Laborers training facility. Its programs began in 1983 with a mission to provide workforce education and training for labor union members and apprentices. Trainees live onsite. The original 1950s flagpole from the former military site remains in use and can be seen here. (Courtesy of D. MacKinnon.)

Jim Thompson sold land to the school district for Kingston Junior High, now Kingston Middle School. He operated an airfield behind the property, and his daughter Jo Nelson still maintains the airfield license. In this photograph, Nelson and her grandmother Henrietta Leyman operate the Nike lookout station in 1950. The lookout stood on the corner of Miller Bay Road and West Kingston Road, and lookout volunteers staffed it in four-hour shifts. Locals referred to this intersection as "Maple Tree corner" until the tree disappeared. (Courtesy of Jo Nelson.)

In the 1970s, oil companies came through Kingston purchasing oil and gas leases. In spring 1972, L.J. Welch drilled a well for Mobile Oil on E.M. "Ed" Arness's land. Arness, seen at left in the image to the left, told Welch he planned to build a home on the cleared land but would "rather have an oil or gas well." Welch offered to paint the top of the rig green to make it less noticeable among the trees, but residents objected, stating, "That's our well . . . we're proud of it." (Courtesy of Suzanne T. Arness.)

Robert P. Smiley stated that he would "like to see that drilling rig . . . put in right behind my restaurant. I'd get a kick out of watching it . . . and I'd sell lots of Smiley Burgers." The drive-in, pictured here, never actually turned a profit. Smiley used it to employ, and thus support, six single-parent households. (Courtesy of the Smiley family.)

The Navy provided housing for military families in a group of homes on West Kingston Road. Kitsap County purchased the site in 2007, and over 150 volunteers led by Rick Lanning and Dave Wetter built the Village Green park on the site. (Courtesy of Rebecca Pirtle.)

Kingston–North Kitsap Rotary erected the picnic pavilion in the playground after a generous donation from member Rea Mowery. A former Marine, Mowery served in World War II, Korea, and Vietnam. He envisioned families gathering, rain or shine, for picnics, parties, and more. Rotary received a Rotary District grant that helped with the playground equipment, and members constructed some of the park benches. (Courtesy of Kingston–North Kitsap Rotary.)

Kingston does not have a World War II memorial.
Local service members are honored in a memorial
at the state capitol in Olympia. The above float
pays tribute to the community's veterans. Those
presently serving are honored on blue star flags
displayed on light posts throughout downtown
Kingston, as seen at left. This Blue Star Banner
salutes Colin Dupont, who serves in the Air Force.
(Above, courtesy of KHS; left, photograph by
Ed Goodwin, courtesy of Nena La France.)

Five

FUN AND WHIMSICAL SPIRIT

The first Independence Day celebrated in the Pacific Northwest took place on July 4, 1841, when explorer Charles Wilkes and his crew joined local tribes for a feast at American Lake in Pierce County. Decades later, the 83 settlers pictured here gathered on an old skid road at East Third Street and Washington Boulevard to observe Kingston's first Fourth of July in 1890, just 10 weeks after the town was platted. The bearded man leaning against the tree is believed to be developer Samuel B. Brierly, posing with many of Kingston's founding families. (Photograph from Eleanor Elkins, courtesy of KHS.)

The photograph above shows townspeople dressed up and gathered for a barbecue picnic at the beach on July 4, 1906. The little girl at front center is Irene Bannister, and W.J. Collins is at right center wearing an apron. In 1910, tourists mingled with the hometown crowd in downtown Kingston, below. Fourth of July bunting decorates the post office and Hyggens store. Present-day Fourth of July celebrations draw up to 35,000 people to Kingston for the traditional parade. (Above, photograph from Linda Amdal, courtesy of KHS; below, photograph from Betty HasBrouck, courtesy of KHS.)

The fire department has historically promoted numerous community events. During the Fourth of July celebrations in the mid-1950s, they supplied a "Duck 'Em" tub at carnivals. In this photograph, two firemen take the plunge in 1957. Vern Stevens is closest to the water, and the other is unidentified. (Courtesy of NKF&R.)

The fire department also drove in the parade. This 1996 photograph shows unidentified youngsters riding in a retired rig. The truck is in front of Smiley's Motel. Mayre Walker recalls that throughout the 1980s, "they would run the parade through town several times, as it was so small, but the streets were lined with old and young." (Courtesy of NKF&R.)

For many years, the Kingston Fourth of July celebration included a carnival. Here, Audrey Dennis appears in costume with an unidentified fellow volunteer in 1957. The carnival raised funds for the ambulance association. (Courtesy of NKF&R.)

Local celebrity J.P. Patches visited Kingston in 1975 to participate in the Fourth of July festivities. He is pictured with an adoring fan, Anne Marie Olson. (Courtesy of KHS.)

This 1960 photograph shows the spectacular fireworks display over Apple Tree Cove, produced for many years by the Firemen's Club. Today, local residents contribute approximately $35,000 annually to continue this Fourth of July tradition. (Photograph from NKF&R, courtesy of KHS.)

Local community leader Mike Wallace initiated many service projects and had a reputation for spontaneous ideas, like the Fourth of July bathtub races, pictured in 1980. First place in the race earned a $40 prize. Wallace knew almost everyone in town, either through his bathtub-refinishing store or his liquor store. Later, residents would name the park at the port after him. (Photograph by Helen Hill, courtesy of KHS.)

The 1989 Fourth of July included a logging contest to see who could perform the fastest timed cut, testing skills and equipment. In the photograph above, two loggers are making a cut while others look on. In 1992, Jack Simmons, below, officiated the slug races, in which participants encourage real slugs with the strategic use of salt. (Both, courtesy of Jerry DeCoteau.)

In 2018, Kingston Lumber observed 50 years of business in Kingston. Owners Tom and Rosalee Waggoner both taught school before buying the business. For decades, their trucks drove in the Fourth of July parades, and each truck bore a name, like "Fanny's Fleet" above. For a few years, the business also entered floats in the parade. The photograph below shows the original Kitsap Lumber location in 1995, at the corner of Highway 104 and Lindvog Road. In recent years, it moved a few miles down the road to a business park on Bond Road. (Both, courtesy of KHS.)

Over the years, civic organizations have planned entertainment for the youngest residents. One example is Tiny Town, a miniature Kingston seen here. Started and trademarked by Mayre Walker in 1992, volunteers erected the wooden structures that replicated the town at Kola Kole Park every Fourth of July. The Fourth of July committee moved the activities to the Village Green park and into tents in 2016. (Courtesy of Tilney Sutherland.)

For over 30 years starting in 1976, the fire department sponsored an annual Easter egg hunt. This child participated in 1979. The tradition continues at Kola Kole Park under different sponsorship. (Courtesy of NKF&R.)

For a time, the Smiley family hosted a large bonfire on Halloween in a vacant lot on California Avenue. Mary Smiley would give each child a free hot dog and cola. Sam Arness would contribute large stumps to keep the bonfire burning. In this picture, Robert P. Smiley and his son Bob are working on an automobile in front of Kingston Community Center, near California Avenue. The community center building was eventually torn down, and a fire station was built on the land, which now houses Kafé Neo and the Firehouse Theater. (Courtesy of the Smiley family.)

The arrangement of stars on the American flag suggests this Thanksgiving pageant took place in the 1940s. Kingstonites have always enjoyed dressing in costume. Kenny Howerton sits on the left. Standing in the first row, second from right, in the majorette costume is Marion Parcells, and to the left of her is Janet Minert. The other participants are unidentified. (Courtesy of Marrion Dennis.)

Prior to television, residents did not lack for entertainment. In 1923, these five musicians dressed up to play the violin and sing. The violinists were Allie Gordon (left) and Charles Van Keuren. The mustached singer in the back on the right is Joe Alexander, and the others are unidentified. A longtime resident reminisced that "the old community center had basketball in the evenings, dances on weekends, and movies on Wednesday nights in the winter sponsored by the sheriff's office. No one had a television until Nelson's Store got one in 1948. Then we would all go over every Thursday to watch." (Photograph from George Andresen, courtesy of KHS.)

Volunteers constructed the community center seen here in the 1930s. The community borrowed money for the windows from the Bank of Poulsbo, which they paid back at 50¢ a month. Members of the community had to pay dues of $1 per year. Residents used the center for public meetings, holiday celebrations, picnics, and parties. During World War II, a deputy sheriff hosted moving pictures. Jack Minert reminisced that "there was also a full basketball court that the kids could use anytime; all we had to do was figure out whose dad had a key and could stay to close up." Minert's mother, Maxine, a school teacher, kept the books for the center. (Courtesy of the Smiley family.)

Originally the site of Whitney's Grocery, Mickey Whitbeck's Kountry Korner store suffered a fire in 1985. He seized the opportunity to rebuild and created a roadside attraction by commissioning a chainsaw artist to carve the Krazy Kreatures (seen here). It was a success, and tourists would stop for an ice cream and have photographs taken with the carvings. For 30 years, the carvings marked the entrance to Kingston on the southwest corner of State Highway 104 and Miller Bay Road. (Courtesy of Kathy Sole.)

When the Port Gamble S'Klallam Tribe bought the Kountry Korner property, they donated the 10 remaining Krazy Kreatures to Tania Issa, who moved them to her store, Kingston Mercantile & Marine. Originally, Whitbeck had commissioned over 10 carvings, but a dragonfly was stolen and another was lost in a property dispute. Once the carvings were relocated, Issa hired the original artist to restore them. For Halloween 2018, Kingston Dental staff designed costumes based on seven of the creatures. Pictured above from left to right are Toni Brianna Comstock, Heather Harrell, Taylor Wall, Ashley Dudkiewicz, Erin Phillips, Sara Couch, and Dr. Sean M. Couch. Pictured below mimicking the ice cream carving is Sara Couch. (Both, courtesy of Kathy Sole.)

Kites Over Kingston is a community event that brings out kite lovers of all ages. Started in 2007, participants need to bundle up since the winds are cold and blustery in March. The above photograph captures a butterfly kite flying high above the crowd. The event Almost Summer attracted several thousand boaters in 2018 to kick off boating season. The winter holiday season includes a Christmas celebration at the Port of Kingston with a fantastic tree and park light display. In 2003, the celebration included the horse-drawn carriage pictured below. (Above, courtesy of Mary Saurdiff; below, courtesy of KHS.)

Six

SMALL-TOWN
VOLUNTEERISM

Volunteerism is the hallmark of Kingston. To join Kitsap Regional Library in 1945, residents pulled together space in the small cafeteria behind the Kingston schoolhouse, now called Kola Kole. Lumber was donated by the Port Gamble Mill, and volunteers built the bookshelves. A card party raised funds for curtains, and support was provided by the PTA. The volunteers pictured here are unidentified. (Courtesy of Kitsap Regional Library.)

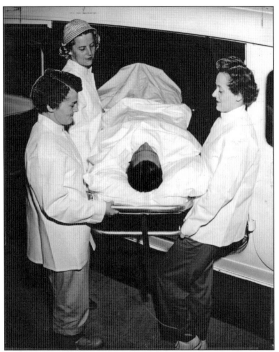

In 1946, the volunteer Kingston Fire Department solicited donations, and the majority of residents contributed $10. The department did not hire its first employee until 1982, when it offered a contract to Chief Paul Nichol. Three businessmen—barber Ray Weaver, bank officer Jerry Orr, and entrepreneur Robert P. Smiley— signed the note to purchase the first ambulance. They subsequently ran the Fourth of July carnival to pay off the loan. The picture at left shows ambulance practice in 1954 with Captain West on the stretcher. From left to right, Irene Nilsen, Lu West, and Pearl Gordon practice their skills. Below, the same women are seen in 1953 protecting the community during daylight hours. (Both, courtesy of NKF&R.)

When needed, soldiers stationed at the Kingston Nike missile site volunteered to assist the Kingston Fire Department. Soldiers and firemen pose in 1956 in front of the Ohio Avenue firehouse. (Photograph from US Army, courtesy of NKF&R.)

Fire Chief Harold "Teen" Elkins complained about the lack of space in the Ohio Avenue Station, pictured here in 1967. He acknowledged, however, that it was better than the first station—an old GI tent. Jerry Kilmer stands outside, while Asst. Chief Nichol is behind the wheel. (Courtesy of NKF&R.)

Voters turned down the first levy to build the fire station that is now Kafé Neo and the Firehouse Theater. The photograph above shows pre-construction signage in 1974. The fire station on Miller Bay Road opened in September 2001. North Kitsap Fire & Rescue now operates five stations. The headquarters (below) houses full-time personnel, a classroom, office space, and training facilities. It also offers a garage large enough to house modern trucks and aid units. Two-thirds of all present-day calls are medical related; of the remaining calls, only two percent are for actual fires. (Both, courtesy of NKF&R.)

The fire department gradually increased its emphasis on prevention. Children found Blaze, the firehouse dog, a popular volunteer. The above picture shows Blaze in 1995, the year after he was donated to the department by the Steele family of Kingston. At right, Blaze looks up at two girls dressed in Dalmatian coats. Blaze became so popular that nearly 100 community members celebrated his 10th birthday, which included cake, a scavenger hunt, and a special puppet show. Blaze's service came to an end when he passed away at the age of 13 on February 12, 2008. (Both, courtesy of NKF&R.)

The Kingston Arts and Crafts Guild was formed in 1980. Member quilters created this quilt representing Kingston as a fundraiser in 1985. Since the winner of the raffle lived in Marysville, the quilters bought it back for $100. The quilt has remained in Kingston ever since, and is now displayed at the Village Green Community Center. The guild dissolved in 1995. (Courtesy of Kathy Sole.)

Local businesswoman Nancy Martin, pictured here, restored the quilt and researched its story. Her community volunteerism has included serving as the Greater Kingston Chamber of Commerce president and as a Village Green Foundation board member. Through her leadership, Martin initiated Concerts on the Cove and Pie in the Park. (Courtesy of Nancy Martin.)

Robert P. Smiley stands in front of Smiley's Auto Service with his family; from left to right are son Bob, daughter Diane, and wife Mary in 1948. Wanting their children to participate, Robert revived the Triple Nickel Boy Scouts Troop 555 in 1951, and Mary began a Brownies troop. In honor of his volunteerism, the Scout cabin in Kola Kole park is named for Robert. (Courtesy of the Smiley family.)

Steele family Boy Scouts all earned the distinction of Eagle Scout. In 1967, Darrell (far right) earned his by retracing the 1889 Press Expedition through the Olympic Mountains. Next, Gary planted 1,000 fir trees at Kitsap Memorial Park in 1972. In 2006, Garrett built the handicap ramp on the Austin-Kvelstad Gazebo in Poulsbo. In 2011, Grann built the cover over the handicap bridge at Bayside Community Church. (Courtesy of Cheryl Steele.)

The Greater Kingston Chamber of Commerce operates a visitors' center staffed by volunteers. Approximately 4.1 million people passed through Kingston as a result of ferry traffic in 2017. Of those, around 5,000 stopped at the visitors' center. The downtown is seasonally welcoming, with hanging baskets and decorated light poles, with volunteers providing all the labor. The group first identified as the Kingston Revitalization Association, but it is now known as the Community Beautification Committee. Pictured in 2003 are, from left to right, (first row) Ron Muell, Karen Ross, Helen Humes, and Kay Peiguss; (second row) unidentified man on ladder, Sally Christy, and Jack Minert. (Courtesy of KHS.)

Begun in 2009, the Port of Kingston's holiday light display models the Bellevue Botanical Garden display. What started small with only four volunteers grew so large that the port's circuit breakers blew in 2013. Now, over half a million LED lights and half a mile of string lights display fish, owls, cranes, whales, a lighthouse, a sea serpent, and more—all powered by separate pedestals. More than 10 volunteers start building new installations and repairing old ones in March each year. (Above, cartoon by Walter Elliott; below, courtesy of Stark Ravenholt.)

The county named the Kingston skate park for former chamber of commerce president Billie Johnson, who advocated for the park. On the south end of Lindvog Road, the park marks Johnson's favorite tractor route. Neighbors remember him cruising on his John Deere, singing off-key, waving, and kicking up his Birkenstock-ed feet. He served in the Marines, worked in construction, and became an ordained Pentecostal minister. His mantra, "Let's all work together and get it done," guided his many volunteer efforts, which included serving on the Kingston Ferry Committee, and several terms as a fire commissioner. (Left, courtesy of Kimberly Jones; below, courtesy of Kathy Sole.)

Since 1999, Stillwaters Environmental Center has protected and restored the natural spaces around Kingston, especially the estuary, salt marsh, and Carpenter Creek watershed. Stillwaters relies on many community volunteers and university interns, connecting students of all ages to the natural wonders around us. Scientific research and monitoring is done with local universities, tribes, and Kitsap County. Pictured here, Ken Patterson (left) and Jonathan Olsen install the interpretive sign at Arness Park. (Courtesy of Stillwaters Environmental Center.)

From left to right, Kiwanians Dick Matthews, Pete DeBoer, and Dave Muller are pictured at a mystery murder theater. Robert "Bobby" Lee, with Mike Wallace and Cy Wyse, founded the Kingston Kiwanis in 1984 to "get Kingston away from its 'wild west of Kitsap County' reputation." The club commits to serving the children of the world. Kiwanis became the first service club to admit women as members in 1986. (Courtesy of Pat Bennett-Forman.)

Kingston–North Kitsap Rotary started in 2004. With the motto "Service Above Self," it addresses needs in the community and internationally. Pictured is the ground breaking for the community reader board on State Highway 104 and Lindvog Road. From left to right are Rotarians Doug Hallock, Clint Boxman, and Jon Sole, with Randy Hanson, owner of Hanson Sign Company, and Dave Wetter of Greater Kingston Kiwanis. (Courtesy of Kingston–North Kitsap Rotary.)

VILLAGE GREEN FOUNDATION

Build a place that connects and strengthens community

Having a community center has always been very important to the citizens of Kingston. The first center was constructed by volunteers in 1930 with materials donated by Pope and Talbot. When Kitsap County purchased the old Bayside Community Church building on State Highway 104 in 1985, the second community center building was founded, and it now houses Coffee Oasis. Though planning for a new community center started before 1990, the community drafted the Village Green Concept Plan in 2001. The Village Green Foundation broke ground for construction in 2015. Below, stakeholders attend the ground breaking; from left to right are JoAnn Cratty, Tomi Whalen, Christine Rolfes, Jill Jean, Sherry Appleton, Jo Pederson, Rob Gelder, Derek Kilmer, Clint Boxman, Mary McClure, Wendy Armstrong, Isaac Anderson, Luke Moreland, Cathy Morris, Nancy Martin, Dave Muller, Kay Peiguss, Don Hutchins, Kendall Hanson, Tracy Harris, and Bill Tsoukalas. (Above, courtesy of Bobbie Moore; below, courtesy of VGCC.)

Above, Clint Boxman, a Village Green Foundation board member and a Kingston–North Kitsap Rotary past president, auctions off pies during the Pie in the Park fundraiser, which raised donations needed to complete and fund the Village Green Community Center project. The event continues and now includes children's games and a pie eating contest. Below is a table of pies made by local bakers, who donate two pies—one for sampling and one for the auction. The record-setting pie sold for $5,000 in 2014. (Both, courtesy of VGCC.)

The Kingston community raised more than $9.1 million for the Village Green Community Center. It has greeted over 200 visitors a day since opening in 2016. The Village Green Metropolitan Park District (MPD) was formed in 2010 by ballot measure to manage the park and center. It is governed by five commissioners: Tracy Harris, Jason Manges, Bobbie Moore, Jim Moore, and Patrick Pearson. (Courtesy of VGCC.)

Kingston Community Solar LLC funded and installed solar panels on the Village Green Community Center in 2016, as seen here. This system generates about 50 percent of the building's electrical usage. The savings reimburse the company through July 2021, when the investors will be paid back, and the system's ownership transferred to the VGCC. At that time, future savings will benefit the MPD and, thus, the taxpayers. (Courtesy of VGCC.)

Kingston Cares was formed in 2013 to address issues facing youth, the homeless, and the poor in the community. In 2014, the group established a severe weather shelter to provide a warm, safe place for people to spend the night. In 2015, the group partnered with Kingston's ShareNet, Rotary Club, and Kiwanis, as well as the Port Gamble S'Klallam Tribe, to assume oversight and expand an existing Food4Kids program to feed students during school breaks. Additional initiatives include a monthly community meal, annual community conversations, and an annual Project Connect Services Fair for low income, homeless, and food-insecure persons. This photograph shows Jennifer Menne (left) and Jackie Shoaf packing Food4Kids boxes. In the background are Diane Tandy-Guerrero and Stan Mack. (Courtesy of Melissa Filben.)

Seven

NATURE LOVERS' GETAWAY

Clark Jackson poses proudly with two deer and two large raccoons after a 1912 hunting trip with Avery Smith, not pictured. Early settlers saw few deer, but many bobcats, lynx, raccoons, and skunks. Present-day residents tolerate deer walking through their yards, and veterinarians advise keeping pets indoors since cougars still run in the greenbelts. (Photograph from George Andresen, courtesy of KHS.)

Mildred Sandahl snuggles a baby bear just found in the woods in front of Sandahl's restaurant on Central Avenue around 1947. As recently as June 2010, Shelly Nolte spotted a black bear on her property at the top of Ohio Avenue. The Sandahls sold the building to the O'Briens, who ran a grocery store there. (Photograph from Rose M. Harrison, courtesy of KHS.)

Pearl Soderberg landed this 25-pound king salmon while fishing in a small boat a few yards off the shore of her President Point home. Early fishermen frequently caught wild salmon this size. Rex Carlaw recalls a Ruth Jaadan Pickerell story of a salmon jumping into her father's boat as he rowed into town. Her father took it home to eat. Soderberg was a local artist, and when her home burned, Jerry Cooper of the Kingston Fire Department rushed into the house and saved her many paintings. (Photograph from Pearl Soderberg, courtesy of KHS.)

Above, Einar Nordberg (left) and Harry Bannister caught fish at Miller Lake across from Wolfle Elementary School around 1926. Rex Carlaw remembers that even in the 1960s, "You were kind of on your own; no doctor, no bank, and no high school. Mostly summer homes. You self-entertained with a rowboat and a bicycle." Below, an unidentified caretaker maintained trails and aided guests at Miller Lake. (Above, courtesy of Cliff Nordberg; below, courtesy of KHS.)

Apple Tree Cove provided great swimming at high tide. Above in 1910, three ladies enjoy the water and each other's company. Below, a 1947 picnic is being held at the head of the cove. In the background is the town's first trestle bridge, on South Kingston Road. (Above, photograph from Betty HasBrouck, courtesy of KHS; below, courtesy of Stillwaters Environmental Center.)

The above photograph shows South Kingston Road when the tide was out. The vertical lines left of center are rollways from the old log dump landing. The 2009 photograph below shows Kolby Waggoner "slurfing" the tube, a concrete culvert that funneled tidewater from Apple Tree Cove under the road. Slurfing involved standing on a skimboard and holding onto a rope tied to the guardrail above the culvert. As shown, Kolby slurfs the flood tide as it rockets out of the tube. Slurfing ended in 2011 with the removal of the culvert. (Above, courtesy of KHS; below, courtesy of Kolby Waggoner.)

A joint venture of Stillwaters Environmental Center, Kitsap County, the State of Washington, the Suquamish Tribe, Department of Fish and Wildlife, and the Army Corps of Engineers was responsible for removing the culverts under South Kingston and West Kingston roads in 2012 and 2018, respectively. Bridges replaced the culverts to improve the fish and wildlife habitat of the pristine estuary and to restore access to the estuary for kayakers and beachcombers. In 2011, the Kitsap County Board of Commissioners officially renamed the South Kingston bridge Stillwaters Fish Passage. (Both, courtesy of Stillwaters Environmental Center.)

In addition to swimming and slurfing, Kingstonites enjoy boating on the water. Using a Recreation and Conservation Office grant in 2014, the Port of Kingston built the kayak storage pictured in the background. The Kingston Sailing Club started in 2015. (Courtesy of Rick Eveleth.)

Bob Smiley (right) is pictured with his sister Diane in 1960. That year culminated six years of racing as a youth. In his later life, Smiley garnered seven national and world speed records. He also continues his father's legacy of support for the local Boy Scouts. (Courtesy of the Smiley family.)

Kingston rarely experiences severe winter weather. However, in 1916, a storm dumped drifts of snow that lasted until April. In 1942, the district canceled school for a whole month, and in 1950, the slough froze over, encouraging ice skating. Jack Minert reminisced about hauling his sled to the top of Ohio Avenue with his friends and sliding to the ferry dock. The arrival of the Nike control site put an end to sledding down Ohio Avenue. Both photographs on this page are undated. The one above shows a house to the left, built in 1912, that now serves as the Mossback Café. The picture below features drifts several feet high outside of Roy's Place. (Above, courtesy of KHS; below, courtesy of Janet Alecci.)

Two women appear to be contemplating a game with a bat and a rock on a ball field in what is now Kola Kole Park. (Courtesy of Tim Burns.)

From 1944 to 1948, Kingston had its own baseball league. It played other local teams on Ed Moon Field, now Kola Kole Park. Dick O'Dell, affectionately called "Digger," batted left-handed and could hit the ball over the fence, whopping cars waiting in the ferry line. Ed Moon, pictured here, taught baseball in the community for over 30 years. (Courtesy of Juanita Moon Martin.)

YOU'RE A SUCCESS at Kingston Jr. High!

Playing field options expanded when Kingston Junior High opened in 1990. For many years, the junior high fields also hosted the Kingston Classic soccer tournament. The school became Kingston Middle School in 2007. (Courtesy of Cindy McKay.)

Voters passed a $60.1 million capital bond in 2001, and Kingston High School opened in 2007. Athletes started with 19 sport options, and within five years, the school claimed multiple state championships. Initially, the fields lacked lights, so the community initiated the GOT2 C 2PLAY campaign. Rotary started its annual golf tournament as a fundraiser for this project. Teams first used the new lights in 2009. (Courtesy of Kathy Pavlich.)

An early resident planted this Camperdown elm around 1905, but plot maps make it difficult to determine who planted it. Jack Minert stands in front of the ornamental tree, which his mother, Maxine, saved when she persuaded crews to spare it during the construction of the Kingston sewer treatment plant. The tree still stands on the Village Green campus. (Courtesy of Lois Minert.)

Homeowners Mervyn J. Williams and his wife, Lois Parcells Williams, planted the Monkey Puzzle Tree at the corner of Second Street and Iowa Avenue around 1960. Mervyn served at the degaussing wharf near Kingston, where he met Lois, who is from one of Kingston's oldest families. Baker Family Telephone Company employed Lois and provided these unique trees to their employees to thank them for their service. (Courtesy of Don Hutchins.)

Arborist Jim Trainer declared the American chestnut planted by Sam Leyman outside of Kingston around 1905 one of the largest chestnut trees in the nation. The tree, seen here behind Jo Nelson, stands 70 feet tall, has a spread of branches about 70 feet wide, and is listed in the American Forests national register. Many larger chestnut trees succumbed to an imported blight around 1900. (Courtesy of Jo Nelson.)

Sonny Woodward remembers the planting of the trees in the median featured here. The money for the project came from a grant and included sidewalks. Woodward and Tom Waggoner were on the planning committee. Tad Parrington completed the work. (Courtesy of KHS.)

According to Sonny Woodward, in 1991–1992, the county was discussing the "Open Space" concept. Woodward was asked to make a presentation, so he and his friends, Tom Waggoner and Joe Schwan, successfully showed the committee why Carpenter Lake should be nominated. Unfortunately, funding failed to materialize. However, after some time, the Trust for Public Lands became interested, and with matching funds from the county, the lake was purchased. At left, the six-to-eight-acre lake is seen in 2011, with its surrounding fringe bog. The picture below shows Tim Burns fishing in Carpenter Creek around 1950. (Left, courtesy of KHS; below, courtesy of Tim Burns.)

In the 1950s, Naomi Libby Elvins pitched Army surplus wall tents on several wooden platforms to make a camp for recreational visits by families. In 1993, she transferred this property to the county, stipulating its use, development, and maintenance. Elvins dedicated the park, now known as Quiet Place Park, to her daughter Catherine Marie (1937–1957). (Courtesy of Ed Goodwin.)

Ed Arness grew up in Kingston, attending school through the eighth grade, since the closest high school was several miles away in Poulsbo. He worked for the Puget Sound Navy Shipyard in Bremerton and logged while buying land that he converted into tree farms. In 1973, he donated land in honor of his parents, Sam and Esther (pictured to the left in the late 1940s), now known as Arness Park. Above, Ed cuts the dedication ribbon in 1978, while his brother Sam Jr. holds the ribbon. (Above, courtesy of Suzanne T. Arness; left, courtesy of Helen Arness Lawson.)

Today, Arness Park is across from the marina. These two giant chairs provide great photo opportunities. Over a dozen such chairs dot the Kingston community. (Courtesy of D. MacKinnon.)

Heritage Park is accessible off Miller Bay Road, one of three heritage parks in Kitsap County. Its entrance leads to multiple trails. Artist Craig Jacobrown painted the mural at the park's entrance. (Courtesy of Ed Goodwin.)

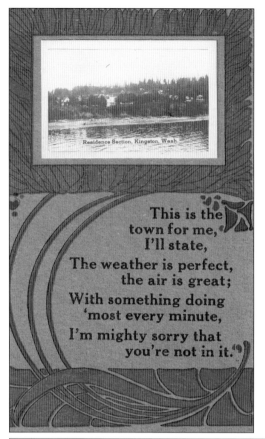

This is the
town for me,
I'll state,
The weather is perfect,
the air is great;
With something doing
'most every minute,
I'm mighty sorry that
you're not in it.

The Mount Zercher postcard to the left captures the sentiment of those who live in Kingston: "This is the town for me." Residents stay for the natural beauty, as illustrated in the photograph below from 2004, looking west from the marina. Individuals and families enjoy the friendly hometown support and the outdoor activities, whether on the water or in the woods. (Left, courtesy of Ed Goodwin; below, courtesy of Mary Saurdiff.)

About the Kingston Historical Society

William O. "Bill" Reynolds remembered riding a Mosquito Fleet ferry and picking cherries at the Owens Cherry Orchard. He did not want that history lost, so he founded the Kingston Historical Society in 2002, with official meetings starting in 2003. For 12 years, the group gathered to share stories. It met and kept its collection of documents, photographs, and artifacts in a basement room in the town community center on State Highway 104.

In 2014, the society became inactive. The remaining Kingston resident, Harriet Muhrlein, held out hope of resurrecting the society, and in 2015 wrote a column for the *Kingston Community News* asking for volunteers to assist her. Jan Bourgeois, Marian MacKenzie, Susan Anest, and Kathy Sole responded and began the task of reorganizing the society. Sole became president, and later, Deborah L.J. MacKinnon became secretary/treasurer. When the community center was sold to Coffee Oasis in 2016, the society moved its collection to a private residence.

Though the Kingston Historical Society does not have a physical presence in town, it has embraced technology and collaborated with other businesses and organizations to fulfill its mission. KHS communicates primarily through its Facebook page, website, and exhibits in local buildings. The society is also in the process of developing an electronic collections database and digitizing its document and image collection. It is now a 501(c)(3) nonprofit organization. The society can be contacted via email at kingstonwahistory@gmail.com, on its Facebook page, or through its website at www.kingstonhistory.org.

This book is not meant to be a comprehensive history of the Kingston community, but rather a celebration of our distinctive community. The society has tried to be as accurate as possible in creating this work, and the source materials listed below were consulted to confirm some information. As with much historical data, we expect that some errors or omissions may occur despite our best efforts. If some are found, please contact us. We are committed to correcting them in future publications.

Bibliography

Bowen, Evelyn T., Rangvald Kvelstad, Elnora Parfitt, Fredi Perry, and Virginia Stott. *Kitsap County: A History*. Silverdale, WA: Kitsap County Historical Society, 1977.

Newell, Gordon R. *Ships of the Inland Sea: The Story of the Puget Sound Steamboats*. Hillsboro, OR: Binford & Mort, 1960.

Osborne, Harold F. *Little City by the Sea*. Kingston, WA: Apple Tree Press, 1990.

Yumibe, Yukie Fukuzawa. *From Cherry Blossoms to Strawberries*. Gorham Printing, 2006.

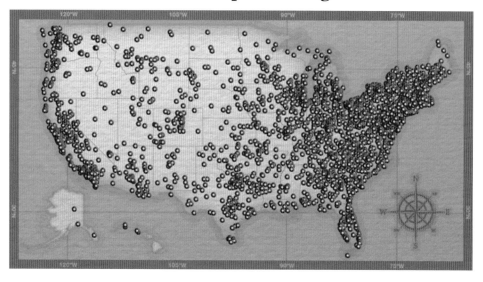